THE GEM THAT BLOOMED

LAKEYA BROWN

Copyright © by 2020 Lakeya Brown
All rights reserved. No part of this publication may be reproduced, distributed, or transmitted in any form without the prior written permission of the author, except in the case of brief quotations embodied in reviews and certain other noncommercial uses permitted by copyright law.
ISBN: 978-0-578-66769-0

Contents

Untitled Note 1
Gems Take Time 2
Seed 3
Where You Need to Be 4
The Unbecoming 5
The Goal 6
Level Up 7
Who Am I? 8
Purposeful Gem 9
To Love Yourself 10
Power to Create 11
The Truth About the Seed 12
Hope 13
I Dare You 14
Next Season 15
Created 16
You Will Lose 17
Shine 18
Innate Sweetness 19
I Can't Make You Grow 20
Best Life 21
Adversity 22

Nicks & Frictions 23

Worthy to Be Loved 24

Approval 25

Flow of Life 26

Rebirth 27

Responsible For You 28

Change Your Environment 29

Separation 30

Bloom Out 31

Day by Day 32

Pieces 33

My Process 34

Gifts 35

In Season 36

Do Not Resuscitate 37

Allow It 38

Imperfections 39

Move Freely 40

Forever Changed 41

Intentional 42

Cultivate 43

Greatness 44

Where to Grow 45

Friend to Friend 46

Weakness 47

Strength to Change	48
Rain	49
Flower	50
Abide	51
Inward	52
Guard Your Heart	53
Live	54
Loyalty	55
Consider it Betrayal	56
Limiting Yourself	57
Misunderstood	58
You First	59
Myths	60
Slow and Steady	61
The Beauty of Failure	62
Dangerous	63
Deceiving Heart	64
Focus	65
Perseverance	66
Similarities	67
Love & Bloom	68
The Art of Falling Apart	69
Master of Nothing	70
Tears	71
Obedience	72

Rare Gem...73

Outgrown..74

Uncut 75

Cocooning 76

Within...77

The Magic of Beginning and Ending 78

Evolve 79

Uncrushable...80

Planted...81

Rise and Grow...82

Manure...83

Zone of Comfort 84

You're Allowed 85

Blindfolded Souls...86

Align...87

Raining Sorrow..88

Purpose..89

The Gift of Solitude 90

Adjust and Readjust..91

Guarded Heart 92

This Journey..93

Changing..94

Wilt, Bloom, Repeat 95

Metamorphosis 96

I Am Gem...97

Go	98
Freewill	99
Human Nature	100
Free Flowing	101
Today	102
Through the Dirt	103
Wildflower	104
Life	105
It Takes Time	106
Pressure	107
Through the Mud	108
Acceptance	109
I Celebrate You	110
For Maximum Growth Only	111
In Full Bloom	112
Dominion	113
Patience	114
Breaking Up	115
Challenged	116
Roots	117
Heart	118
Sticks and Stones	119
Potential	120
I Stand with You	121
Increase Awareness	122

Undeniable	123
Dear Gems	124
The Antidote	125
Recovery	126
No Announcement	127
What You Feed	128
To the Flowers, To the Gems	129
Learning	130
Solitude	131
Dear Growing Pains	132
Goodness	133
Messy Growth	134
Silence	135
Meant to Be	136
A New Day	137
Endure	138
Worthy	139
Bloom Again	140
From the Ashes	141
Cheer	142
Value the Gift	143
Thoughts	144
Still Healing	145
Afraid	146
Rejection	147

For the Gems	148
Take Love and Light	149
Self-love	150
Closure	151

Untitled Note

A Gem is one who chooses to move from the cycle of survival, into the cycle of thriving and fulfillment of their purpose. We were all created for a purpose and our purpose is intertwined. We all struggle and fumble around, whether silently or publicly, we're all taking nicks and bruises. We all go through seasons of growth and pruning so that we are better equipped for what we are ultimately destined to fulfill. The Gem that Bloomed shares that we are not alone in our seasons. I hope that you feel encouraged to keep pursuing healing and purpose, to become the best version of yourself.

Gems Take Time

Gems take time.
Respect your process.
You need patience,
effort and consistency.
Be intentional and stay
close to the things that help you bloom.
Put in the work,
heal, pray and bloom with purpose.

Seed

A seed is only a seed,
It will not take on its true nature,
it will not root or flower if you don't first, plant it.
Allow the burial and the uncomfortable darkness
because, in the end, the character
and the truth of the seed cannot be silenced.
It cannot remain buried.
In the end, its light and destiny must manifest.

Where You Need to Be

I hope that once you train your
mind, body and soul to align,
your heart will be right where it needs to be.
Securely rooted in an environment that nourishes
and feeds you from now until eternity.

The Unbecoming

There is a portion of your growth that will require you to unlearn all that you have learned.
This is unbecoming.
In your unbecoming, there is a heightened level of vulnerability, a terrifying level of nakedness.
Lean into that fear.
The unbecoming of thoughts, feelings,
and behaviors that dictate you, is meant to unearth
who you are and reveal to you what you were
truly created and purposed for.

The Goal

The goal is simple.
Looking at others will only complicate it.
Choose to root down and stand tall,
stand tall and flow freely, bending and adapting,
making friends with the wind
and trusting the magic of every direction.
Understanding that it means you no harm or malice.
Formed only to push you towards the light
and harvest infinite growth.

Level Up

There are levels to this life
and you will need to know this.
The levels are not created equally.
Beauty and destruction is present within each,
allowed only to push you to where you
were born to be.
Each level requires a different pressure,
a different state of being uncomfortable,
a different mind,
a different heart,
and a different you.
At the point to which you believe you've made it,
just know that there is more.
More pushing, more pressure, more purpose.
Each level will require another burial
and another birth.
Each will be painful but even more painful
if you don't lean into it with the understanding
that you're going to win.

Who Am I?

Who am I?
I wish I could tell you and be certain.

I mean is anyone ever certain?
I know that I am always waking up and showing up,
ready to evolve and thrive.
Ready to do what I am created to do, in this season.
I am evolving, I am becoming.
A brief answer may satisfy you
but it would cause me to become uneasy.

You see, what holds is this,
every second produces a moment to
become someone different.
I am complex and simple.
I am who I was at birth, at the age of 5,
at the age of 16, and who I am now.

Every moment in collusion with purpose
to reveal the dormant gifts inside of me.

Purposefully manifesting into all that
I was created to be before all of the voices
made me fearful, before all of the experiences
encouraged me to become doubtful.

Purposeful Gem

She is a rare gem, set apart.
She is not driven by power nor prestige.
This gem is not driven by money or tangible items.
She does not crave to belong
but she aches for experiences.
She is driven by purpose and love
from the Creator of her very being.

To Love Yourself

To love yourself means
to break up with every thought,
every person, every behavior,
every feeling and every intention that does not reflect
and deposit love in its most unadulterated form.

Power to Create

It all begins and ends in your mind.
You have the power to create
and you equally have the power to destroy.
Choose wisely.

The Truth About the Seed

They sold us a fairytale.
There are no magic seeds that one could plant today
and expect a full bloom tomorrow.
All seeds take time.
It takes love, it takes effort and consistency.
No matter how rich and forgiving the Earth is,
it takes years for a gem to formulate
in the belly of the earth,
and even longer for it to reach the surface.
Flowers have a natural order taking multiple seasons
to germinate, surface and unfold.
So don't let the lack of results and no's
and slammed doors deter you.
When it's your time nothing can stand
in the way of your full bloom.

Hope

The darkest places give way to the brightest spaces.
No matter how toxic or draining a season may be,
it creates an environment,
conducive for growth and change.
There is always hope,
you just have to train your eyes to see it,
your thoughts to know it
and your heart to believe it.

I Dare You

No truths only dares,
I dare you to move.
Move out of that place that has buried
and suffocated you.
Move from the place that has held you
in a state of bondage.
I dare you to move past those thoughts
that keeps your mind confined
and fixed on negativity.
Go where people say you can't and won't.
Move.

Next Season

Everyone won't make it to your next season.
Some were meant to bury you
and some to water you.
No matter how much you want them to, they can't.
You'll try to bring them along,
you'll try to include them but everyone can't go.
Everyone won't endure the drought season,
the reaping and sowing season.
Let them go and wish them well.

Created

I want to be the flower that grows wild and fruitful.
Attracting the sun,
drinking in water and adapting to each season.
Attracting those who are loved and nourished
and those who need to be loved and fed correctly.
I wasn't created to be tabled or be a trophy.
I was created to be lush, daring and free.

You Will Lose

Yes!
You will lose but if you focus on the things
that will be lost, you'll remain the same.
You'll miss the things that you've gained
and become resistant to the process of loss.
The purpose of this loss is to make room
and prepare you for the abundance of new blessings.

Shine

You will never know how truly great you can be
if you keep dimming your light
so that others may feel comfortable.
Reflecting light is your birthright.
Sometimes the criticism of others feels like the truth,
it will feel like you're condemned.
We believe from our level of perception.
If you listen, feed on and digest what others say,
it's because internally you already
don't feel worthy enough to shine.

Innate Sweetness

I bet no one ever told you that even before the moment
of conception you possessed sweetness.
A sweetness that was commanded to grow

and so it grew, and grew, and grew.
And at the moment your mother pushed
and you passed through the canal into the light,
this moment was one of your sweetest.
As you pass through the season of burial and renewal
don't allow the bitterness of this life,
to rob you of your sweetness.

I Can't Make You Grow

I can throw fertilizer on you
but I cannot force you to grow,
nor can I grow for you.
I can provide all the elements
that are needed for growth
but you are not a project, you're human.
You are fully capable of taking ownership of your life.

So I offer you sunlight, you can share mine.
As the rain waters my soil it will roll to your roots
and satisfy your thirst.
That's what kindness is about,
that's what love for all mankind looks like.
I offered you the elements that I have
and I expect nothing in return.

Best Life

If you constantly dwell in the what if's,
if you are constantly waiting until things are clearer,
you'll miss the magic in the small moments
that want to change you from good to great.
If you're waiting for perfection you're not living.
Love. Live. Thrive.

Adversity

Everything has a purpose.
You can bloom without adversity and pain,
but how will you influence the ones
who are attached to your purpose?
Will the breath be sweeter
and rewards be enjoyed to its depths?
Will you shine as bright as you were meant to shine?
You need the burial, you need the pain, the rain,
the sun and every conflict the Earth may ensue.
Embrace them.

Nicks & Frictions

When you were created,
you were created from the inside out.
Don't let little nicks and the friction of stones
diminish your value.
It's only an external distraction, created to permeate
and contaminate you internally.
Refocus, refresh, and refuse
to be destroyed from the inside out.

Worthy to Be Loved

You don't have to be anyone else.
You don't need to bend and break
to understand and learn this lesson.
You are worthy of love and to be loved.
You don't have to search,
it will come and it will feel like the sun.

Approval

What you don't like,
have enough courage to change it.
But make sure that the change

comes from a place of self-love,
because people will seek to change you
without even knowing what they like.
Wouldn't it be a shame to change
the things that make you unique
for the sake of another person's approval?

Flow of Life

Today in your solitude stop and shift your focus.
Your growth is not for anyone else to understand,
but for you alone.
When the time has come
and your growth is no longer invisible,
when you're unable to be suppressed
they'll bear witness.
Just grow with the flow of life.

Rebirth

In the moment that you realize that you are worthy,
you are forever changed.
In that moment you are reborn
and your mind is renewed.
In that moment and every moment that follows,
you will always choose you.

Responsible For You

It won't always make sense.
You'll feel out of step with the people
you once felt in tune with,
because sometimes you outgrow
people who choose to remain in places
that prey on the mind of the complacent.
Release the guilt,
you are only responsible for you
and your own growth.

Change Your Environment

When the growth is minimal
and you begin to doubt its existence,
consider a change of environment.
Silently remove yourself from everyone
and everything that burdens or hurts you
more than they show their love for you.
All that is chaotic and chokes the peace from your soul,
release it by moving on.
Leave malice and unforgiveness behind
and press on to better places,
better places that will lead to better days.
Illuminating the path to attract better people and things.

Separation

There is a mourning that happens
during the growth process.
You shed the people, the places and the things
that you thought would last forever.
Your beliefs and values are challenged
and the things that attached itself to your existence
are shaken and sifted, separating dirt from gem.
Whether it was healthy or diseased
you'll miss them because if it were up to you,
you'd stay and never say goodbye.
Separation is necessary for elevation.

Bloom Out

We want to grow up and bloom out
until it's time to fold our sleeve
and do the internal work.

Turning inward is frightening but, evolving is essential.
Don't allow fear to paralyze you in any level of growth.
Once you've exhausted your purpose in each phase,
you are ready to move on
and begin the internal work again.

Day by Day

Some days I have it, some days I fail at it.
With each day and from moment to moment,
I choose to love myself
and honor my journey of growth.
I choose.
Some days I fail, some moments even.
But I keep loving myself regardless,
because no one will choose me like I will choose me,
and no one will love me better than I love myself.

Pieces

Even in broken pieces you have value.
In pieces you still will bloom,
you are purposed and chosen.
There is a love that you can obtain
if you let go of the expectations
and fears you've placed yourself under.

My Process

This is my re-birth and I'm unapologetic.
I am evolving and I won't slack up
because you feel threatened.
If I evolve past you that's because I was meant to.
I won't be afraid or slow my progress.
I've begun to enjoy this process because
I'm falling in love with becoming my true self.

Gifts

When you take your eyes off of your goal,
when your mind is not sound
and your intentions are not set, you will falter.
It will never be about how fast you get there,
it will never be about who has the most or least.
Your life is strictly about you
and how you can take what God has given you
and how you use it to serve, encourage,
uplift and inspire others.

In Season

Society will pressure you to rise
and bloom prematurely.
They will pick you and place you on display
before you are fully blossomed.
Bloom only when you are ready,
bloom for no man's glory.
Bloom because this is your time
and your season.

Do Not Resuscitate

I'm learning the power of DNR.
Not friends, not family and not relationships.
If it's not surviving
and it has the tendency to harm my growth,
I am making the choice to let all things
that do not serve a purpose flat line.

Allow It

Whatever falls away, allow it.
Whatever leaves, close the door behind it.
If it pulls away when you push,
if it separates and floats,
with open arms allow it to go.
Allow everyone their freedom,
you are too much of a gem to force your value
onto others who refuse to acknowledge it.
Just because they refuse to acknowledge you
doesn't mean that you lack value.
You were forged with love and purpose
to reflect truth, love, peace and light.

Imperfections

The greatest thing about being a gem is that your
imperfections are what make you beautiful.
Don't be afraid or ashamed of them,
your imperfections are the very gifts
that feed nations and endow generations.

Move Freely

Yes, it's difficult
but with adversity you'll find relief.
Don't let yourself get stuck,
move freely in every season.
Whether difficult or easy nourished or unfertile,
it is your innate responsibility,
to move freely and grow.

Forever Changed

Once you figure out your purpose
once you understand that your being here
is a collection of small miracles,
once you figure out who you are and whose you are
your life is never the same,
it's forever changed.

Intentional

If I remain budded and tightly closed,
I am not living in my purpose.
If I keep my back to the sun
and my roots half planted,
I am out of alignment with my purpose.
I was created for such a time as this and so were you.

Our purposes are entwined,
so let us turn our face to the sun.

We are purposed,
chosen to bloom and bloom intentionally.
We will no longer remain closed and comforted,
when blooming is our destiny.

Cultivate

What you plant will grow if you tend to it.
So nurture it well and love it.
If you want it to be all that it has
the true potential to be, put in your time,

put in your effort, be consistent,
and watch it flourish into its full purpose.

Greatness

I've come to realize that I was made for greatness.
It does not matter if you value the gifts
that are within me.
I was created to till, to sprinkle the seeds of love
and to water that which I've invested
my time and energy in.
My validation and self-worth was established
and rooted before you had a thought of me.

Where to Grow

The inability to stay where you are,
that feeling of being uncomfortable
is your soul screaming,
"try something new".
Listen to the uneasiness within.

Try changing your environment.
It is possible that you can no longer grow here.

Friend to Friend

My Friend,
these trials were not meant to kill you,
they were meant to strengthen your roots
and make you bloom.
The rain came to strengthen you
where you've grown weak,
to balance the toxicity of the environment,
you've been planted in.
The winds increased to tear away
the chaotic weeds that seek to encamp you.
Root and bloom, bloom and root
until your purpose has been fulfilled.

Weakness

The power is not found in how well you control the situation, anyone can manipulate and control.
The power is not in how well you recover after life has held you in its hand like a mortar
and crushed with its pestle.
Your power comes from your willingness to relinquish all control, with the understanding that our strength
can only be made perfect when we are strong
enough to confess our weakness.

Strength to Change

There is no truth to, "because I'm stuck right now, this is now my fate."
You have the strength within to stand up,
to change your thoughts and your behaviors.
You can learn new habits that keep you growing.
You just have to decide on changing.

Rain

The rain will come, don't be afraid.
It was created to aid your growth.
The rain will surely come,
sometimes as gentle as first steps
and other times as hard as a stampede.
Whatever the amount,
it will be the right amount to help you evolve.
You will not drown, your roots will sustain you.
You are not alone,
the rain will fall on you and I just alike.

Flower

If you don't take the time to heal,
you'll never have time.
Healing brings uncomfortable shake ups
and avoidance is easy.
You'll experience some height,
but never know what you can grow to become.

Your leaves will begin to bloom
but eventually wilt and turn brown.
You will be purposed to be in your blooming season,
but you won't flower.
Your roots will no longer take in the nutrients because
the toxicity of unresolved issues will clog them.
Take it at your pace,
no matter how slow the process seem.

Abide

It won't be today, maybe not even tomorrow.
But one day you will wake up
and just feel it in your bones,
that this is the day that you release the loads
that were never meant for you to carry.
You will feel the emotions
and heaviness pass through you,
close the door as it exists.
You may cry and maybe even want
the unhealthy load to return.
The choice is yours, choose to abandon the load
and dance shamelessly in the fields of freedom.

Inward

There is a growth that occurs
when you are loved right.
That type of growth can only begin
when you turn inward
and decide to love yourself.

Guard Your Heart

You were created and born whole.
You've taken some chips, licks and bruises along the way, so naturally you feel broken and partial.

However, with time and work
you'll learn to practice more self-care.
You'll learn forgiveness.
You'll learn to guard your heart
because a casted arrow hurts the worst there.

Live

Live out your purpose,
be all that you were created to be.
Don't hoard your purpose but find the drive to fulfill it.
Your purpose isn't for you alone,
you have the power to affect nations.
You have an obligation to generations.
So decide to share your gifts.
Unfold, flower and prosper.
Except everything that is for you,
even when it seems hard.

Loyalty

Loyalty is not always to another person,
sometimes loyalty is to yourself.
The misuse of loyalty will keep you planted
in areas you know that you should have uprooted
and moved on from.

Consider it Betrayal

If you have to cross the line for that relationship,
you should know that you're betraying yourself.
If you have to compromise your morals,
your values and your soul,
ask yourself, is it truly worth it?

Limiting Yourself

I've decided to begin this journey.
The journey to freedom will begin with limiting myself.
I am leaving the people and places that only value me
when I can fulfill their needs,
in order to dwell within the places
that I feel most loved and appreciated.

Misunderstood

Some gems are created for the purpose of
understanding, so rarely will we be understood.
There is a loneliness that sets in.
It requires constant maintenance
in order to keep us growing
and reflecting love and light.
It is bitter-sweet, and there is beauty and pain
that comes from being misunderstood.

You never really feel at home,
no matter how comfortable
and loving that place feels.
But don't falter, we are not alone,
there are those who understand us,
our paths are destined to intertwine.

You First

It is not fair to you
to heal, water and protect others
and neglect yourself.

You deserve the same love
and affection you freely offer them.
Invest in yourself, everyone else can wait.

Myths

There is a myth about growth.
We've been told that growing
is only for the spring season
and for this very reason some have become stuck.
We are to grow, to rise and bloom in all seasons
not just the spring but summer, fall and winter.
No one can dictate your growth.
True growth begins from the inside out.

When it is your rising time we will see
the manifestation of your inside work.
Even in full bloom the growth is still underway.
You still need water, sunlight, and oxygen,
you still need nourished roots to maintain the bloom.

Slow and Steady

Gems need time to form,
to fall apart,
to go through times of purification.
Gems need time to bloom.
Take all the time you need
and at the right time you will burst forth.

The Beauty of Failure

Pick your head up
it's not about how well you start,
this marathon of life is about how you finish.

You are not defined by your failings,
but by each moment you fall,
and choose to rise.

Shake the dust off and begin again.
Success is a series of failures collected one by one
and worn as a crown.
Success is when you're unashamed for the world
to see that failing was the main ingredient
in your recipe for success.

Dangerous

This season is my most dangerous bloom.
I cut through rocks and defy all rules.
This bloom is dangerous
because I'm no longer taking your opinion
into consideration.

Deceiving Heart

When my soul said walk away,
my heart said try harder.
I listened to my deceiving heart.
That was the moment I undermined my worth
and in the end I learned to value my intuition
and myself.

Focus

Sometimes we focus too much on the bad,
maximizing and making things appear worse.
Refocus your mind, think about the reality of it all.
Now focus on the good.
Focus on all the possibilities that are waiting on your
changed thoughts, so that they can overtake you.
Rather than believing the inner dialogue
"I'm such a mess",
celebrate how far you've come
and how many victories you've won.

Perseverance

Persistence through the discomfort is key.
You are allowed to slow your pace.
If the growing is scary, pace yourself.
Rest in the unfamiliar places.
Shake away fear or it will grow like restless weeds
ready to choke away life.
Learn how to be planted
and to flow with the breeze of life.
Learn to master peace at each stage in life.
Knowing that each will bring you
right where you are destined to be.

Similarities

Gems, flowers,
art and the human race.
We are more similar than we are different.
We are both born out of darkness into the light.

Do not fear the exposure of light,
the darkness will keep you small.
There will be seasons when you will grow
strong and tall, and other days when you will wilt

with just enough strength to turn your face
and receive nourishment from the sun.

Love & Bloom

Life and death can't occupy the same space
just as one can't be both healthy and unhealthy.
We can't thrive in toxic places.
Toxic places breed illnesses, which breeds sick people.
Let go of the toxicity.
If you hold on it will only hurt worst.
It will confuse you and reject your growth.
If you let go, the beautiful that is trying to bloom
from within you will take root
and when the time is right the beauty
will grow in place of all that was once barren.

The Art of Falling Apart

Before something great can grow,
before I can be all that I was created to be,
I had to fall apart.
The roots were good but the environment was foul.
I couldn't grow so every petal needed to fall
stubbornly from its bud, so that the planter could
uproot and find me a better place to grow.
My roots were always good.
Learning to bloom from the millions
who came before me,
the ones who make up my lineage
and the ones who do not.
Dying so that I may have better than them,
ending so that I could begin and flourish.

Master of Nothing

There are moments when you believe
that you've mastered the hard aspects of life.
That is not so.
There are times when I think I've mastered peace.
When I think I have gotten used to the
uncomfortable place of shifting, moving and changing.
When I've mastered the art of love,
the complexities and delicacies of communication.
Life has a way of stripping away the walls
and showing you that you're no master,
only a student, preparing for the test.

Tears

Even if it's my tears,
I water my soul daily.
I feed it what is necessary
to thrive and endure.

Obedience

Give yourself time, you will evolve.
You will come forth and bloom.
Blooming will yield blessings,
and when you bloom correctly
all of creation will benefit
from your obedience.

Rare Gem

She is a rare and dangerous gem.
She is not driven by power or prestige.
She is not motivated by money or fame.
She is a rare gem, motivated by purpose
and longing to bloom from the inside out.
Longing to experience the love
and excellence she was created to enjoy.

Outgrown

You will reach a certain point of growth
where you won't fit into the places you once did.
You will outgrow who you once were.
You won't be able to keep the company
that you use to keep.
So evolve without resistance
knowing what is meant to be, will be.
Knowing those who want what's best for you will
understand and encourage your freedom.

Uncut

To the one who looks for grandiosity,
who looks for the finished product,
you'll go unnoticed.
Wish them well and be on your way,
because there are others who will see you with clarity,
and will find joy in the natural beauty of the uncut gem.
Your rarity and worth will be cherished,
you'll be protected and loved entirely.

Cocooning

I'm ok.
I'm not sad, I'm not sick I'm not missing or lost.
I know exactly where I am,
strategically tucked away.
I am in my cocoon.
I can't grow big, I can't go strong,
I can't grow wings to land on purpose,
without drinking in the goodness of solitude.

Within

The world surrounding you,
will never quiet down.
Master the art of quieting your heart,
master quieting your thoughts.
When your inner world is silent,
your spirit can grow
and your heart will learn to dance in tune
with the sweet cadence within itself.
Your thoughts feel safe,
and become your own again.
If you align within, you clear the path
and give light to all that is trying to bloom.

The Magic of Beginning and Ending

Inhale is to begin as exhale is to end.
As easy and automatic as it is
to begin a breath and end, such is life.
We must learn to do the same in our situations.
We must believe that for every situation life delivers,
there will be a clear beginning and an end.
Relinquish control and follow the natural order
and flow of things.
There is a time to fight and there is a time to give in.
Trust the beginning, and the ending,
knowing that we are all constantly evolving.
Growth will bring worry so learn to be at peace.

Evolve

You will reach a certain point within your growth,
where you won't fit into the places you once did.
You will outgrow who you once were,
to take shape and form of who you are meant to be.
So evolve.

Uncrushable

Dear Gems,

All though you feel the pressure from all sides
and pieces of you have chipped and detached,
you are uncrushable.
You were designed to evolve,
so embrace the constant changes.
Be patient, you are still becoming
who you are purposed to be.

Planted

Perhaps you've struggled because you've searched for
all you desire in the wrong nectars.
You have sought outside of your own environment.
What you seek is already inside of you.
It's been there, dormant since birth.
Turn inward and watch,
you will find all that you need.

Rise and Grow

You will rise, you will grow.
The winds will howl and you'll fight it as if you're foes.
Rest and save your strength,
because the wind is the beginning of growth.
The rain will pour and your petals will soak,
some may even break,
they were dead anyway.
Your roots will strengthen if you choose to be still.
You will rise, you will grow.
You will hurt for a moment, but you cannot fold.

Manure

Abandon your grudges you needed it to happen.
The path you chose was too shallow
for the depth of your purpose.
Thank them all, for the rich dirt
and fertilizer they threw on you.
It was purposed and allowed
in order to grow you up.

Zone of Comfort

Your comfort created the illusion of a
land flowing with milk and honey.
Meadows of flowers and exotic things
fill this zone of living.
Birds are chirping and dragonflies soar
above blades of grass.
But you've rested here too long
and your comfort zone has ceased to produce growth.
And when your mind understands this,
you'll wipe your eyes like a child waking from a deep
slumber seeing that all that is here is staleness.
The milk and honey has spoiled, birds no longer sing,
dragonflies have no fresh grass to lie,
and butterflies have floated away
in search for better days.

You're Allowed

Set yourself free from the unrealistic expectations
created from childhood, and others.
You are allowed to grow, make mistakes
and be imperfect.
You are allowed to be human
and let the masks disintegrate in whatever direction.
You are intended to grow inside out.
You'll find the sun,
you'll find all the necessary resources.

Blindfolded Souls

It is not your fault,
some simply walk through life with blindfolded souls.
Some only able to perceive force fed
perceptions of love, beauty and success.
Closed off to the true virtues of life,
lacking the understanding that everything has beauty.
Even with its oddities things, people,
and places are deserving of a chance.
Don't allow them to stifle your growth.

Align

When you overthink
you propel yourself into the future
and freeze yourself in the past.
Overthinking creates fear, worry and doubt.
You are unable to live in the present
where you truly belong.
Accept here, accept now.
Choose to stop picking over thoughts
as birds gathering loose seeds.
You were created for such a time as this.
Align your heart and will with the Creator's heart
and will for your life.

Raining Sorrow

Sometimes sorrow falls like rain,
but it is necessary for us to grow.
So don't be afraid of tears,
you'll outgrow the pain
if you do the work.
You will survive it all.

Purpose

If caged birds still operate in their purpose
how much more responsibility do we have
to keep to the path that is laid before us.
To operate in our own lanes,
while journeying towards purpose.

The Gift of Solitude

Solitude grows self-awareness.
You have to be able to leave behind
all the people, thoughts and places
that keep the noise and chaos alive.

Adjust and Readjust

You are allowed to change as much as you need to
in order to grow into the person you are destined to be.
You need no one's permission, only yours.
Adjust and readjust until it all feels right to you.
They don't have a say in how long
it takes you to adjust.

Guarded Heart

My heart is not a paper that you can fold,
unfold and refold at your convenience.
My heart is strong, well-guarded and valuable.
Worthy to be loved the right way, worthy
to be filled with goodness and respect.
My heart is priceless,
and only a person who has done their own heart work
will understand such value.

This Journey

The things that stick to the walls of your heart
and cling to the matter of your mind.
The backwards teachings that have kept you small,
and the negative thoughts that have kept you
from breaking through the dirt, release them.
On this unnerving, fickle and intoxicating journey make
sure you embrace the process of growing.

Changing

I am changing, I can sense it.
The things that once made me afraid,
no longer scare me.
In fact, I dare it to try to overtake me.
I'm changing, less afraid of failing,
less afraid of fading away.
I'm changing because I can see myself clearer.
I have relinquished the perfection
and though chaos and forces are surrounding me.
I feel less pressure and I see the light.

Wilt, Bloom, Repeat

You are allowed to wilt and adjust,
wilt and bloom, bloom and wilt again.
Repeat this process as many times as you need,
in order to be all that you are called to be.
Give yourself permission
to change in any and every way,
to heal and become purposed.

Metamorphosis

You're stuck, I know.
It happens from time to time.
It could possibly be because we were taught that the butterfly goes through only one metamorphosis.
The truth is we are much like the butterfly
but we are also like the flowers,
the sunrises and sunsets,
we are like the billions of stars
that cycle in tune with the Creator's voice.
To survive it all, you will need to morph as many times
as you need to in order to come out truly happy.
Cocoon and seek solitude,
as many times as you need to.

I Am Gem

I am gem,
I am flower.
I am turning to drink in the sun and reflect its light,
glowing from the inside out.
As dragonflies graze and butterflies lay.
I'm showing up each day regardless of threat
and negative feelings.
Purposed to be vibrant and feeding to all.
I am gem, I am flower.
I am standing in my God given power.

Go

Go where you're loved,
where you feel at peace,
where you're energized,
joyful and celebrated.
Give yourself permission
to separate from the people
and things that serve no purpose.
Go where you're loved and peace is reciprocated.

Flow and grow where you are appreciated.
Be intentional with your love, peace, and words.

Freewill

Toxins and nourishment surround us,
the bad and the good.
Life is happening in the midst of it all.
There are some who will fold
from the pressures of life,
and others who will unfold.
Whichever you choose,
know that free will is yours.

Human Nature

It is our human nature to find comfort
and in finding comfort we become stagnant
and eventually feel stuck.

There are important lessons in becoming stuck.
Pay attention to the process.
Push through.
Grow and allow what was created to flow,
flow as freely as the wind.

Free Flowing

I have to leave now.
You can't come, you have to stay here.
This may be your blooming place,
but I need to shift,
I need to be transported
to an environment that allows for growth,
that allows me to be all that I was created to be.
I have to go where light, life and love grows freely.
The journey to that place may be long,
but I can't stay here.

Today

If today all you did was root down,
turn your face to the sun and breathed
in order to quiet your heart and mind,
that is enough.
Rest in the abundance of that self-care.

Through the Dirt

You can't break through the dirt
and grow upright if you don't first
free yourself from the opinion,
bondage and gunk others used
to weigh you down and bury you under.

Wildflower

I love wild flowers,
they don't ask for permission to grow.
Wildflowers, they just do what they were created to do.
They grow.
They are uncompromising, living in their truth,
and when they are plucked and tossed to the side they die, giving life back to the soil in order for other wildflowers to grow.

Life

In life what often causes us to become stuck
is the belief that because our foundation
is designed to be solid,
everything else in life must be set in stone.
But life is fluid, uncertain and constantly changing,
moving us backwards to launch us forward.
It moves us left and then right,
life flings us up and slams us down,
taking us low, in order to launch
us into our destined excellence.

It Takes Time

It takes some time,
some growing and stand stills,
some collapsing and struggled sprouting,

but somehow you will end up
blooming like you were destined to be.

Pressure

You cannot bloom
without the pressures of the earth.
Without it you remain dull.
The pressure activates and agitates
and only when you persist through its pain,
will you spring forth in purpose.

Through the Mud

There will be times when it gets foggy and murky.
Sometimes all we can see
is the ugliness of our situation.
Sometimes your lenses may become out of focus,
adjust your view.
Through the mud blooms lilies but if you focus on the muck you'll miss the transition to beautiful.

Acceptance

You look good, you feel lighter,
you breathe freely, and love better when
you accept the ugly you cannot change.
Accept the growing pains
and lessons with open hands.

I Celebrate You

For the days you kept walking and shining
with no clue if you were doing it right or wrong,
I celebrate you.
For the days you kept walking, showing up
and trying, that's bravery.
I celebrate you.
To rise when you've been trampled
and to keep moving when it seems
as if your petals have stopped forming requires faith,
I celebrate you.

For Maximum Growth Only

Roses, like the soul knows what it needs to grow.
It knows just the right amount of nutrients
that will heal you from the inside out.
Stop manipulating and sabotaging your growth.

You have been filled
and toiled for maximum budding.
The old dirt will mix with the new dirt,

don't be shaken, ashamed or afraid.
Whether good or bad it'll all work in your favor,
to provide maximum growth.

In Full Bloom

In full bloom
one cannot simply bloom without first being planted.
Your purpose must first be dormant,
in order to be activated
and reach its greatest destiny.

Dominion

Today I did nothing and felt no guilt.
I took my towel and spread it along the manicured grass
and laid with my back against the ground
and belly facing the sky.
The sun licked my skin like a playful dog
does his best friend.
It felt good to lay and breathe,
peacefully inhaling and exhaling.
For a few moments the earth and I were in harmony.
She was kind to me offering support and strength,
and I was kind to her offering love and life.
Today I did nothing but let the earth embrace me while
I embraced her.

Patience

Be patient and at peace with yourself.
You are in no rush to get here or there,
you are in no rush to get to the other side.
You are calm, you are healing,
you are forgiving, you are unfolding.

Breaking Up

I'm choosing to break up with you,
I'm setting you free.
No it's not you, it's me.
I've changed and I'm no longer the person
you used to know.
Growth has spread to every corner,
height and depth of me.
I'm breaking up with all expectations
others have set for me.
I'm breaking up with the patterns and pathologies
that have been internally poisoning me.

Challenged

You will be met with challenges.
You will rise and you will root,
you will lose petals and even wilt.
You will be met with thorns of the first frost.
It may prick you or even entangle you,
but you will not be overtaken.
Rise and root in good soil and although it may look
and feel unbearable and unnecessary,
you will gain infinite strength
when you relinquish your need to be in control.

Roots

My strength is in my roots.
You can trample me, pick me or mower me down,
but I will grow back.
Not right away, but when the time is right
I will bloom more beautifully than before,
stronger than before.
Although your intentions were to destroy me,
it was for my good.
You pruned me.
Thank you.
You helped me grow better,
you helped me grow with grace and excellence.

Heart

Stop letting people touch your heart
with their dirty hands.
Guard your heart jealously, honor it more
and watch it beat stronger.
Watch your life unfold and take on
its rightful meaning.

Sticks and Stones

They'll see who you are now but ignore you,
they'll go back to your mistakes and pick at your
insecurities and flaws to keep you small.
Let them throw sticks,
let them throw stones,
let them throw dirt.
Gather those sticks and build a fire
that will burn away the impurities of your land.
Use the dirt to grow and the stones
to build boundaries around your garden of peace.

Potential

They told you what you lacked
because they saw the value within you.
If they buried the seeds with lies,
then no one else would see.
If no one else could see,
then no one else could water and if no one watered you,
then no one would feel the need
to provide nourishment.
In their ignorance they didn't realize
that seeds require burial for growth.
They didn't know that some seeds don't need others
for their watering and nourishment.

Do not be afraid,
the sun will shine because that is its purpose,
to nourish all below.
There is enough water within you to produce growth
and internal nourishment.
Just as the mud produces lilies and concrete, roses,
applied pressure and dirt produces gems.

I Stand with You

For all the times you wanted to fall apart and you did.
For the times you needed to fall apart but you couldn't,
because falling apart would summon the vultures
and predators to eat the seeds
that needed extra time to take root,
I stand with you.
It takes courage to open up and be vulnerable.
To remain soft and not turn to stone.
To allow the natural order of things to continue to
progress and grow without manipulation.
I stand with you.
In spirit, back to back, hand in hand to help prop you up
when this journey gets rough.

Increase Awareness

Life is too short to spend being at war with yourself.
Spending time with you,
increases self-awareness and self-care.
Learn to navigate through your mind
and pull up every negative weed
planted by dream and purpose killers.
Learn to live in peace with yourself.

Undeniable

To the ones that bloomed without being watered.
To the ones who overcame every adversity
and weathered every unforgiving season.
To the ones who burned down
and somehow managed to blossom with more peace,
love, and virtue, you are rare.
You are undeniable.

Dear Gems

Dear Gems,

The growth that you allowed to encompass your life
has left me breathless at times.
Every time I thought you would bow out in defeat,
you've taken a knee to rest,
then you came back standing tall.
Your bravery and consistency,
I've watched and repeated in my own life.
Your walk encourages me.
I'm rooting for you Gem.
Continue to root down and grow stronger.

The Antidote

How sweet it is to know
and understand that the tears
that I cried in the past was the water for my soul,

the antidote for the disease,
which prolonged my healing.
Confirming that all I needed was placed inside of me
before the day of my conception.

Recovery

Always being strong and ok is exhausting.
Solitude is a place created for recovery.
You are free to cry there, it is safe.
Safe to fall apart and not worry about
putting the pieces back together.
No worries about which mask to wear.
Vulnerability is acceptable and required
to be still and empty out every impurity
that does not grow you,
so that it does not poison your purpose.

No Announcement

When you begin to blossom
it needs no announcement,
it needs no applause.
This growth isn't for anyone else,
it is for you.
Turn your face to the warmth of the sun
and silently bloom.

What You Feed

Feed your dreams.
When you're busy feeding them with hope
and positivity it starves your fears
and dries up the reservoir of insecurities.
Feed all that you have envisioned for your life.
Have faith and grow it strong.
It will fluctuate but keep feeding it.
Believe that you have what it takes.

To the Flowers, To the Gems

Shout out to all the roses growing through concrete,
the sunflowers and wildflowers
unapologetically flowering.
Shout out to all the lilies blooming through the mud
and to all the gems pushing through
the pressure and dirt.
You are deserving of love,
you are deserving of peace and joy.
May these things flow to you
and abundance surround you.

Learning

Life is a series of learning, unlearning and relearning.
Just because it was taught to you,
doesn't make it right.
At any moment you can choose what serves you.
You can choose to remain stuck in unhealthy cycles
or you could embrace the process of
learning, unlearning and relearning,
until what you feed your soul, mind, and spirit aligns.
Choose bravely.

Solitude

When you are silent,
when you are in a season of solitude,
unafraid to look inward, pluck up every weed
and neutralize the toxic waste,
you are ready.
Ready to rise from the depths
and widths of the earth.
Pushing and wading through all lava, molten and sulfur.
Unafraid of the purifying fire
that gives light to your rebirth,
to your goals, dreams and purpose.
This is the day you set your intentions.
This is the moment that you become
the Gem that bloomed.

Dear Growing Pains

Dear growing pains,

I will endure you.
I am thankful for your lessons on flourishing.
What will fold, will fold and what will flourish,
will flourish.
Every situation and every obstacle teaches us resilience.
It teaches us to make better choices and decisions,
to take nothing for granted and nothing personally.
Thank you for helping me in my process.

Goodness

You are worthy of love
and every good thing that will overtake you.
You are worthy of experiencing peace in your spirit.
You are worthy of peace of mind.
You are worthy of not living in constant fighting.
Release all that does not value you,
serve you, or add goodness to your life.

Messy Growth

Growth gets messy and uncomfortable.
When you think that you've learned to prepare
for the impact, when you think you've mastered it,
the uneasiness grows.
It's scary but it is what we are all designed to do.
Nothing unearths purpose like pain and discomfort.
I'm invested in my growing,
I'm invested in my healing,
I'm invested in discovering my purpose.

Silence

There is a season of silence that occurs
after a seed is planted.
Darkness overtakes the seed and solitude is essential.
In this season of solitude water will flow to you,
the sun will shine on you,
and oxygen will find and befriend you.
You need not do anything, just be still.

Meant to Be

There are times when we feel overwhelmed with the thought that we've missed out on people, places and things.
Everything that is meant for you, will find you.
You are right where you're supposed to be.

A New Day

Today is different.
I am setting my intentions, nothing will be the same.
I can't grow in the environment that I was planted in.
Today I am transplanted to a new place,
mentally, spiritually and emotionally.
Today is different and I welcome the change.

Endure

My petals may seem withered
and to you they may appear damaged,
but my roots are strong.
Made to dig down, made to endure it all.
Although the colors fade and my petals may wither,
this is but one season and it all serves a purpose.
Tomorrow may bring a new season
and I will erect again, so please worry about you
and don't pluck me up,
I am purposed.

Worthy

You don't get to decide whether
I am worthy of blooming.
I am the only one who can decide this.
My purpose and my intention is to bloom
whether you water me or not.

Bloom Again

I've lost my petals
I've crumbled and conceded
all because I lost you.
I'm shedding the layers
that were tethered to you,
I've won back my strength to bloom again.

From the Ashes

The Phoenix is celebrated because it burns down
completely and resurrects from its ashes.
The flower is scolded and shamed
if the elements dare burden their petals.

To the flower,
burn down, wilt and be still.
There is victory, even when it looks and feels like defeat.
Rebirth is unique for each individual.
Rest in the security of the darkness,
the exposure and light will come soon enough.
Stand tall, wilt and burn down.

Your ashes will blend and the ground
will be tilled, purifying and cleansing the land.
You will bloom better than before.
Stand taller than before, be healthier
and flourish greater than before.

Cheer

No one will ever cheer for you
like you cheer for yourself.
Clap for you, shout for you, show up for you,
support you, honor you, love you
and most importantly, be complete within yourself.

If you attach your worth or complete it with someone
else, if they decide to leave
they'll take it with them and never look back.
Be solidified within.
That way you could never allow anyone else
to tally up your worth.

Value the Gift

Whatever you treasure, you make room for.
You feel obligated to protect it.
You choose to nourish it, and speak life into it.
Don't let others value your gifts
more than you value them.
In the wrong hands they'll exploit
what God has entrusted you with.
But in the right hands, they take nothing
without filling it back with value.

Thoughts

Being intentional with your thoughts is important.
You create your world with your thoughts.
Empires have risen and fallen
all because of one thought.

Still Healing

There is no place,
no relationship, thing or magic void fillers.
People, places and things were not made to heal you.
Healing is your choice.
You will need to set your intentions.
You have everything you need within.
It's okay if your wounds are still fresh,
if they are still sore and you're grieving.
It's okay if they won't close,
it takes work and self-care.
They will close.
Be patient with yourself, you're still healing.

Afraid

It's alright to feel afraid,
breath through it, move through it.
In the end you will see that it wasn't real.
The fear was only there to make you turn around
and run back to the warmth of comfort.
Move through it, even if you are afraid.
At the end of your comfort zone lies your purpose.

Rejection

We dread the disapproval of others.
Even when you've reach the sense of
"I've arrived",
you still fear that you will be rejected.
The truth is, beautiful things are rejected daily,

not because they aren't worthy,
but because they cost a lot.
Abandon the shame that is attached to rejection.
Rejection is necessary to clear the path
for those who are worthy.
Let their rejection define them and not you.
Bask in your self-acceptance.

For the Gems

You were formed in the lowest of places.
Not all survive the burial,
not all survive the pressure,
not all survive the changes, bumps and bruises.

Not all arrive to the surface and bloom for harvest.
But you, you fearfully made gem,
you were created so that others would
know that they could be strong and courageous.
You were created for a purpose.

Reflect on the many battles you've won.
You have survived all that was laid before you.
Remain focused.
Even on the days that defeat drape around you
like the cape of condemnation,
defeat is not your final destination.

Take Love and Light

If my journey agitates you
and my growth offends you please, step away.
I cannot stop my process to assure that
my necessity of evolution is within the bounds
of the permission you've allowed me.
If this new heart, new mind, new soul
and elevated worth offends you,
you are not hostage here.
Please take a bow and walk away.

Take with you love
and light for your very own journey.

Self-love

Do you know what self-love is?
It is discovering you and then setting your value.
Self-love is not compromising or discounting yourself,
even when people walk away.
Self-love is healthy boundaries.
It is setting your mind and your heart,
it is choosing to stand up and applaud for yourself,
when others do not.
It is having an unwavering position about your worth
and refusing to lower the set standard.
Self-love is the ability to sit alone with your thoughts
and self and have a good time.
It can only be found if you search within.
Then and only then,
can you affirm that you were always worthy of love.

Closure

There are things that you'll want to address
and as bad as you do,
some things are better left with no closure,
and no conversation because it will change nothing.

It will only cause you to become stuck.
Move on.
It won't be easy but it is necessary.

Some things you just need to release
and be alright with,
you don't always need closure.
Sometimes walking away
and moving on is the only resolution you need.